Presented to

_____

By

_____

Date

_____

2-17
Lexile: _____

AR/BL: _____

AR Points: _____

To my freckle-faced brother, John David Streib,
who knows the joys of heaven, and
can join in eternal Psalms of praise
with his heavenly cello . . .
beside King David and his harp.

My deepest thanks to Jeannie Harmon,
my editor, teacher, and friend.
He brought us together to serve Him
and whispered Psalms to our hearts.
S.C.

In loving memory of my parents,
Ruth and Francis Garvin,
now living with God in heaven
and forever living in my heart.
E.G.

Chariot Books is an imprint of ChariotVictor Publishing
A division of Cook Communications, Colorado Springs, Colorado 80918
Cook Communications, Paris, Ontario
Kingsway Communications, Eastbourne, England

PSALMS FOR A CHILD'S HEART
© 1997 by Sheryl Ann Crawford for text and Cook Communications for illustrations.

Designed by Andrea Boven
Illustrated by Elaine Garvin

First hardcover printing, 1997
Printed in the United States of America
01 00 99 98 97   5 4 3 2 1

Psalms
for a
Child's Heart

Sheryl Ann Crawford
Illustrated by Elaine Garvin

Chariot VICTOR
PUBLISHING
A DIVISION OF COOK COMMUNICATIONS

Dear Parents,

Worship, praise, forgiveness, understanding God's love for us—all important aspects of our Christian experience. But how do we convey these key concepts to our children?

David took a simple approach as he watched his father's sheep. He visualized the God of the universe fitting into his everyday experience—God was a shepherd in the same way that he was a shepherd. David not only described God in a frame of reference that he and others knew well, but his words became his expression of praise or his prayer to God Himself.

Sheryl Crawford, author of Psalms for a Child's Heart, *has taken eight selected Psalms from the Bible and put them into words your child will love and understand. Elaine Garvin has added illustrations of kids in real-life situations so that your child will be able to relate God's words to his or her own experience.*

As your child grows to understand more and more about God, he or she will grow in the ability to express praise and worship to God. With this foundation, your child will develop a relationship with the Creator that will last a lifetime.

The Editor

CONTENTS

Psalm 1: *The Right Way to Live* 8

Psalm 8: *My Wonderful God!* 16

Psalm 23: *God Cares For Me* 22

Psalm 32: *God Forgives Me!* 30

Psalm 62: *God Is My Strength* 36

Psalm 96: *My God Is King!* 42

Psalm 100: *I Will Praise You!* 48

Psalm 139: *God Knows Me!* 54

THE RIGHT WAY TO LIVE

Psalm 1

I am happy, God, when I don't listen
to things that wicked people say.
Their words show they do not love You.
They want everyone to listen to their advice.
"This is what you should do," they say.
Sometimes they want me to listen, too.
But I won't listen to them, God!

I am happy, God, when I don't go
where wicked people go.
They do bad things and like to cause trouble.
God, You call this sin.
They want others to do bad things, too.
"Come with us and be our friend," they say.
But I won't follow them or do what they do!
I will only follow You, God!

I love the Bible–Your Word–O Lord.
Your wise rules teach me
the right way to live.
I think about them throughout my day.
Sometimes it's hard for me
to do what is good.
But wherever I am, I can say,
"Help me to follow You today, Lord."

And at night in my bed, when all is still,
I remember words from the Bible.
I whisper them in the dark.
Then my thoughts are filled with You.
"I want to follow You tomorrow," I pray.
For when I obey You, God,
You make me strong inside.
You give me courage to do what is right.

Those who obey will be like a beautiful tree.
One that You planted by a clear, flowing river.
Its roots go down deep into the earth.
It will grow and grow, mighty and tall, full and green,
with delicious fruit for all who pass by to eat.
The fiercest wind cannot move it!
In the cold winter snow, that tree will still grow.
Even the hot summer sun cannot harm it.
Nothing can hurt the tree You planted.
I want to be like that tree, Lord,
growing strong and beautiful for You!
Then the good plans that You have for me will happen!

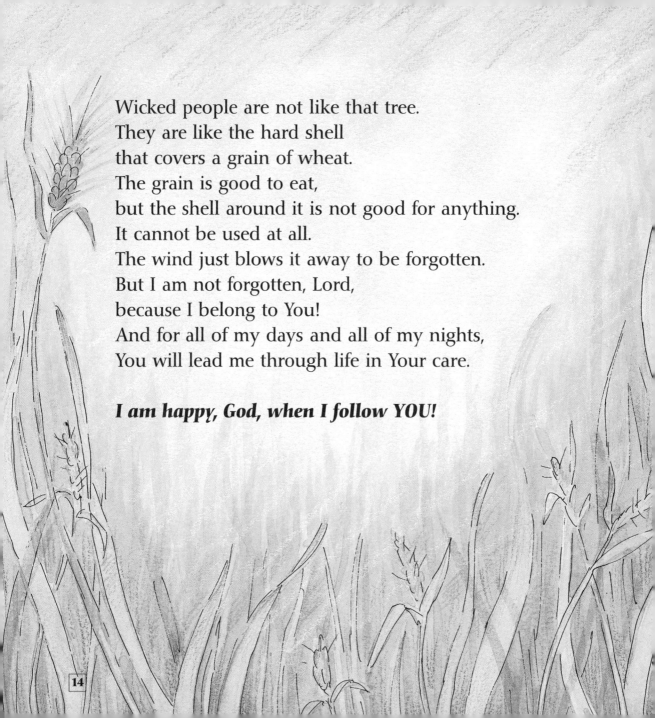

Wicked people are not like that tree.
They are like the hard shell
that covers a grain of wheat.
The grain is good to eat,
but the shell around it is not good for anything.
It cannot be used at all.
The wind just blows it away to be forgotten.
But I am not forgotten, Lord,
because I belong to You!
And for all of my days and all of my nights,
You will lead me through life in Your care.

I am happy, God, when I follow YOU!

MY WONDERFUL GOD!

Psalm 8

O Lord, You are *my* God.
Of all the names that ever were, or ever will be,
Your name is the most wonderful of all!

You love to hear us sing happy songs of praise.
Our voices fill Your throne room!
When people who do not love You
hear us praising Your name,
they do not even want to speak.

When I look into the night sky,
I see what You have made
with Your powerful hands.
I see the stars like twinkling jewels.
No one could count them all.
I see the glowing moon, golden and round,
giving light from afar.
But when I see the sky and moon and stars,
     I feel very *small*.
They are so *BIG* and I am so *small*.
Do You see me, God?
Then I remember that You made *ME*, too.
The same God that made everything, made *me!*
I am not too small for You to love!

God, You made the heavenly angels
to worship and serve You.
Then You made people.
You made us to love You, God!

You created every kind of animal,
and made us masters over them all–
sheep and horses, cows and pigs,
every animal that I could name.

You made the wildest jungle creatures–
ones that I would never want to meet–
all the fish that swim in the sea,
and all the birds that fly.
What a great and mighty God You are!

O Lord, You are *my* God.
Of all the names that ever were, or ever will be . . .

Your name is the most wonderful of all!

GOD CARES FOR ME

Psalm 23

Dear Lord, You take good care of me,
the way a kind shepherd cares for his sheep.
You give me the things You know I need,
and always do what's best for me.

You give me a warm bed to sleep in,
and watch me through the night.
    If I were Your lamb,
    You would find the softest grass
    for me to lie in.
    I could sleep all night and not be afraid,
    for You would watch over me.

When I am hungry,
You give me wonderful food to eat.
	If I were Your lamb,
	You would lead me to the greenest pastures.
You give me water when I am thirsty.
	If I were Your lamb,
	You would take me to a clear, cool stream.

Lord, knowing You makes me feel
good and safe inside.
I love to do what pleases You.
If I am in a scary place,
	or all alone,
		or in the dark,
I know that You are with me.

Lord, You are right next to me.
It is like You are holding my hand.
I don't need to be afraid at all.
     If I were Your frightened lamb,
     You would pick me up
     and hold me tight.
     You would carry me to a safe place.
When others are unkind to me,
and it seems as though I don't have a friend,
I know that *You* love me.
Lord, Your kindness to me will never end.

Every morning when I wake up,
You are there, Lord.
You will spend the day with me.
And you will be there
even while I sleep at night.
There will *never* be a moment
when You will not be with me!

Lord, I belong to You,
just as the little lamb in the shepherd's arms.
Someday I will live with You in heaven,
and it will be our home together . . . always.

I love You, Lord!

GOD FORGIVES ME!

Psalm 32

I feel happy, Lord, because You take away my sin.
You don't stop loving me when I do bad things.
It's as though You wash my heart
and make it clean inside.

When I do something I know is wrong,
I sometimes try to hide it.
My sin makes me sad, and I don't feel good inside.
It is hard to laugh or even smile.
But You are there, God, waiting to forgive me.
Waiting . . . waiting . . . waiting!

Then You whisper to my heart,
and I know what I must do.
I tell You how sorry I am, and You forgive me.
Lord, You erase the bad things I've done–
It's as though I hadn't done them at all!
And even though I sometimes choose
to do things that make You sad,
You still love me.

I know You will help me do what's right.
Your Holy Word teaches me how I should live
when I am small . . . until I am old.
You will be my heavenly teacher.
Every day and always, You will be my guide.
Please help me listen to Your words and obey You first.

It is sad for people who do not love You.
They have many troubles.
They do not know that You can forgive them.
But I know You, God,
and I feel Your love wrapped all around me!

You forgive me, Lord.
So I will be happy and sing with a glad heart.
You take away my sin and make me clean inside.
I feel happy from my head down to my toes!
Sometimes I could SHOUT,

Thank You, God, for forgiving me!

GOD IS MY STRENGTH

Psalm 62:5-8

When my days are filled with sadness,
    who can I talk to?
When I see trouble all around me,
    where can I go?
When I am worried or afraid,
    who can help me?
I will go to *You*, God,
for You are my Father in heaven.
Only You can give me a quiet feeling,
    deep down inside,
    deep in my heart.
    It is *peace* from You.

God, You are like a giant rock
that stands as tall as a mountain!
Earthquakes may try to shake it!
Floods may rush around it!
Mighty winds may blow against it!
But *that* rock will *not move.*
　　　It will not crumble.
　　　It will not fall.
That rock is a shelter;
a safe place for anyone who goes there.
That is the rock *I* will go to!

Lord, *YOU* are my *STRONG ROCK!*
    I will go to You
    when I am sad,
    or troubled,
    or worried, or afraid.
I will go to You anytime, God.
    You will be my safe place.
    You will be my shelter.
    Nothing can move You away from me,
    for I am Your child!
Only You can give me a quiet feeling,
    deep down inside,
    deep in my heart.
    It is peace from You.

Lord, You are my STRONG ROCK!

MY GOD IS KING!

Psalm 96

Sing a joyful song to the Lord!
Sing that He is GREAT and GOOD!
Sing that He is KING!
Sing it to a friend or for everyone to hear.
If I could sing about Him to the whole world,
 I would tell them that the Lord
 can take away every sin!
 I would tell them the Good News, again and again!
 Every child and every grown-up
 from the farthest part of the earth
 must know the great things God has done!
 And every voice in every tongue
 should praise His name!

But many people do not know
that He is the *only* God.
They pray to things that cannot hear them.
I will pray to the one true God,
who made the sky and heavens above.
Look up and see what God has made!

Because He is King, the whole world should say,
"No one is more wonderful and powerful
than our God!"
There could never be enough words
in any language
to tell how great and mighty our God is.
I will bow down to my King.
He is the wise ruler of all.
And nothing can take away His power!

The skies are bright with joy!
The stars shimmer with gladness!
Mighty ocean waves *crash* and *roar*
that God is great!
Golden fields wave in the wind
to their wonderful Maker!
Trees of the forest reach up to Him,
and rustle their leaves in songs of praise!
For someday the Lord will come back to earth.
And He will make all things right and good!

Sing a joyful song to the Lord!

I WILL PRAISE YOU!

Psalm 100

I will use my voice to praise You, Lord!
With a glad voice I will say,
"You are King over all the earth!"
With a happy heart I will sing to You, Lord!
Sometimes I will lift up my head
AND SING WITH ALL OF MY VOICE!
Sometimes I will bow my head
and sing softly to You, like a prayer.
I can sing about You with my family.
I can sing about You with my friends.
I will always have a song
in my heart for You, dear Lord!

I will praise You with thanksgiving
for all that You do!
I will thank You at church.
I will thank You at school.
I will thank You outdoors,
      at the beach, in a tree.
I will thank You at home,
      when I eat, or when I go to bed.
I WILL THANK YOU ANYWHERE!
I will thank You on good days,
and even on bad ones . . .
because You are still *my* God.

51

I will thank You for Your *goodness!*
>   You forgive my sins!
>   You are my closest friend!
>   You are my helper!
>   You are *GOOD*, dear Lord.
You are good for more reasons than I could name!

I will use my voice to praise You, Lord!
With a glad voice I will say,
>   "You are my King!"
>   "You are my Maker!"
I will sing with a happy heart to You.
I will thank You for Your goodness!
I will praise You over and over, Lord!
For Your love for me will last forever!

I will praise You!

GOD KNOWS ME!

Psalm 139

O Lord, You know everything about me.
You see and understand what I am like
as no one else can.
When I sit or stand, play or rest, laugh or cry,
whatever I do, wherever I go,
Your eyes are on me. You know where I am.

You already know what thoughts I'll be thinking,
even before I can think them!
And Lord, before I open my mouth to say a word,
even a *whisper* . . .
You know what I am going to say.

O Lord, how wonderful it is that You understand
everything there is to know about me!

God, Your presence is all around me,
in front of me, where I am going,
behind me, where I have been.
And Lord, You are with me even now.

Is there any place where You would not be?
If I could travel through space to the moon
and beyond,
You would be there.
If I could dive to the deepest part of the ocean,
You would still be with me!

You would guide me safely.
If I cannot see because of the darkness,
God, You will still see me.
Not even the darkness can hide me from You!

Lord, before You made me, You knew my name.
You planned every special thing about me.
You chose the day I would be born,
the color of my eyes and hair,
the sound of my laugh, even the way I smile.
Every single day of my life was known to You.
You wrote them in Your Book,
even before I took my first breath!
Thank You, dear God,
for the wonderful way You made me!

Lord, You are always thinking about me.
Every day. Every hour. Every minute.
If I tried to count Your thoughts of me,
there would be more than all the grains of sand!

When I close my eyes at night to sleep,
You are there.
And when I wake up in the morning,
You are the first One to see me
because You never left.
O Lord, You know everything about me.
You see and understand what I am like,
as no one else can.

Thank You, Lord!